Made in United States
Orlando, FL
05 October 2022

23020773R00067